'/02

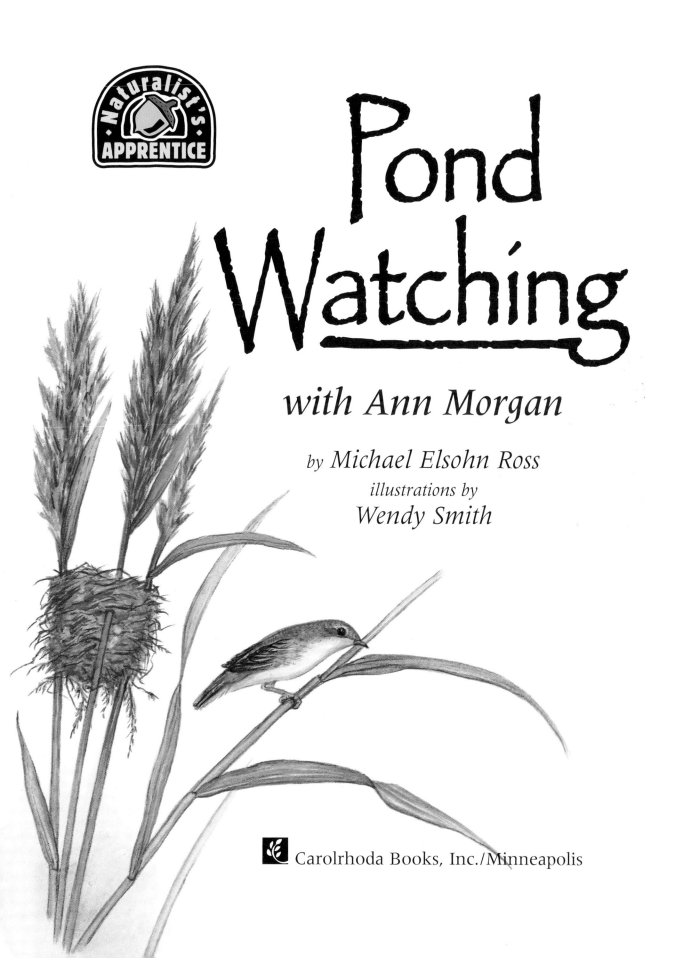

Naturalist's APPRENTICE

Pond Watching

with Ann Morgan

by Michael Elsohn Ross

illustrations by
Wendy Smith

Carolrhoda Books, Inc./Minneapolis

To my water-exploring partner, Nick—M.E.R.

To my parents, Margaret and Clarke, for their love of nature, and to Christopher for his loving help—W.S.

The author wishes to thank Patricia Albright of the Mount Holyoke College Archives and Special Collections, Elaine Engst of the Cornell University Library, Mrs. Robert Kenyon, and Mount Holyoke alumni Bessie Boyd, Isabel Sprague, and Ruth Lowy.

All photographs in this book appear courtesy of The Mount Holyoke College Archives and Special Collections, South Hadley, Massachusetts, except: Courtesy, New London County Historical Society, Inc., p. 6; Courtesy, Division of Rare & Manuscript Collections, Cornell University Library, pp. 11, 16.

Carolrhoda Books, Inc.
A Division of Lerner Publishing Group
241 First Avenue North
Minneapolis, MN 55401 U.S.A.

Website address: www.lernerbooks.com

LIBRARY OF CONGRESS CATALOGING-IN-PUBLICATION DATA

Ross, Michael Elsohn, 1952–
  Pond Watching with Ann Morgan / by Michael Elsohn Ross ; illustrations by Wendy Smith.
    p. cm. — (Naturalist's apprentice)
  Includes bibliographical references (p. cm.) and index.
  Summary: Describes the life and work of Ann Haven Morgan, who studied, taught, and wrote about the animals of ponds and streams and the importance of an ecological approach to conservation.
  ISBN 1-57505-385-3
  1. Morgan, Ann Haven, 1882–1966 Juvenile literature. 2. Freshwater biology—Study and teaching—Activity programs —Juvenile literature. 3. Zoologists—United States—Juvenile literature. 4. Women zoologists—United States—Juvenile literature.   [1. Morgan, Ann Haven, 1882–1966. 2. Zoologists. 3. Freshwater biology. 4. Women—Biography.] I. Smith, Wendy, ill. II. Title. III. Series: Ross, Michael Elsohn, 1952–   Naturalist's apprentice.
QL31.M775.R67 2000
590'.92—dc21   99–24953
[B]

Manufactured in the United States of America
1 2 3 4 5 6 – JR – 05 04 03 02 01 00

Contents

WATER ARUM

Chapter 1
Nature Child

Are you a water watcher? Have you ever peered into ponds or gazed at streams? Perhaps you've spied water striders skating across the glassy surface of a pond or glimpsed turtles diving to safety. Maybe you've been buzzed by zooming dragonflies or entertained by croaking frogs. Do you have questions about pond life? Have you ever wondered how animals breathe underwater or why dragonflies patrol ponds? Imagine exploring the watery world by becoming a **naturalist,** or student of nature.

Over a century ago, a young girl named Anna Haven Morgan roamed her family's Connecticut farm, searching for bugs and poking into flowers. Born on May 6, 1882, Anna was the first child of Stanley and Julia Morgan. Anna's brother, Stanley, and her sister, Christine, were several years younger than she was, so Anna spent a lot of time alone. She liked to wander, and her parents gave her the freedom to explore the fields and forests near their home in Waterford. Like other parts of New England, the land was dotted with ponds and streams. Anna discovered salamanders and turtles, dragonflies and damselflies, and water fleas and crawdads. Little did she know that she would one day be well known for her studies of **aquatic,** or water-dwelling, life.

What's a Pond?

Many people think that a pond is simply a miniature lake. Water naturalists, however, define a pond as a small body of freshwater not more than 12 to 15 feet deep. A pond is shallow enough for sunlight to reach all the way down to the bottom, so rooted plants such as water lilies often grow across an entire pond. The depth and size of a pond may vary greatly at different times of the year. Some ponds dry up completely during droughts, or periods without rain. Ponds provide homes for a wide variety of plants and animals, from duckweed and sedges to snakes, birds, insects, and fish.

Williams Memorial Institute

As a teenager, Anna attended the Williams Memorial Institute in New London, Connecticut, not far from the family farm in Waterford. In the early 1800s, few women received much education. Most girls went to school for a few years, then married and raised a family. But over the course of the century, schools and colleges for girls were opened by people who believed women should have the same educational opportunities that men had. Families who wanted to educate their daughters could send them to schools like Williams—if they could afford it. Anna was lucky to have parents who supported her thirst for knowledge.

Although Anna had the chance to get a good education at Williams, she couldn't learn much about the aquatic creatures she loved. In fact, when she discovered animals in ponds, in streams, or along the seashore, she had trouble learning their names or anything else about them. During the late 1800s, there were few nature guides for young people. Stories about animals were easy to find, but their facts weren't always accurate. Field guides with colorful pictures of plants and animals didn't exist. Fortunately, Anna was a keen observer. This skill enabled her to learn firsthand from nature.

Wet Tour

Have you ever thought about touring the watery world of ponds and streams? Would you like to meet unusual creatures such as the whirligig beetles and horsehair worms that Anna got to know? Check out the nearest pond or stream. If there aren't any in your neighborhood, perhaps your folks can take you to visit one. **Warning:** Water can be dangerous. Visit a pond or stream under adult supervision. Beware of slippery rocks, fast currents, deep water, and polluted or dirty water.

Supplies
✔ notebook
✔ pen or pencil

What to Do
✔ Sit at the water's edge in a comfortable place where you can see beneath the surface.

✔ Look for shadows and movements in the water. These are clues to the presence of animals. Can you spot any water bugs, fish, or other critters?

✔ Make a list of the different kinds of animals that you see. If you don't know their names, just describe them.

✔ What kinds of plants can you spot? Describe them in your notebook. If you're looking at pond plants, can you see any that are rooted in the bottom?

✔ Do you have any questions about what you see? Honor your questions by writing them down. Your curiosity may lead you to more explorations.

WHIRLIGIG BEETLE

Choosing a Field Guide

Unlike Anna Morgan, you can learn about nature from both a good field guide and your own observations. A field guide to ponds and streams will help you identify all sorts of aquatic creatures and understand their habits. Check your local library or bookstore and follow these tips when choosing a guide:

✔ **Illustrations vs. Photos**
Photos are attractive, but a drawing or painting may show more details than a photo. A book with illustrations and clear diagrams can be a big help.

✔ **The Complete Aquarium**
Using a guide that shows a wide assortment of **species**, or kinds, of aquatic plants and animals is like peeking into a well-stocked aquarium. The more information you have on a wide variety of plants and animals, the less baffled you'll be when you meet the uncommon ones.

✔ **Easy Operation**
A guide with clear pictures, descriptions, and maps will be easy to use. The more time you spend searching for basic information, the less time you'll have to observe and explore.

✔ **In the Pocket**
A book that can fit in your back pocket or knapsack is just the right size. An encyclopedia of aquatic life is fine for use at home, but who needs to be weighed down by books on an outing?

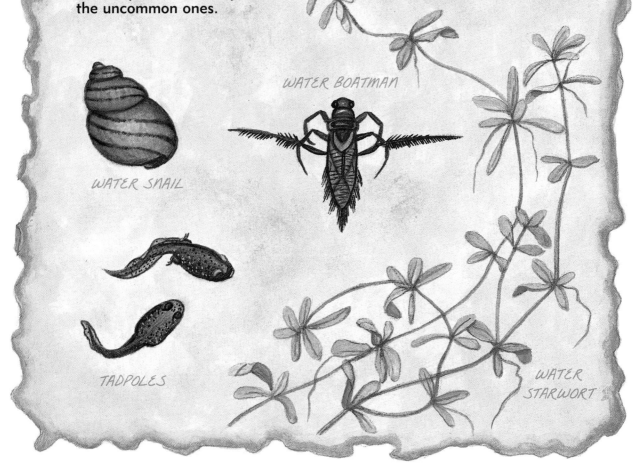

WATER BOATMAN

WATER SNAIL

TADPOLES

WATER STARWORT

Chapter 2
Study Nature, Not Books

Anna did well enough at Williams to get accepted at Wellesley College, a private women's college in Massachusetts. She began her studies there in 1902. Though it was a privilege to attend a school like Wellesley, Anna found the experience as restrictive as the petticoats and corsets that her fashionable classmates wore. The college had too many rules! Students weren't supposed to stay out late, take long walks off campus alone, or even go to the nearby city of Boston.

Anna, who had always enjoyed her freedom, rebelled against the rules and roamed as she pleased. Not only did she disobey regulations by going alone to Boston, but she even attended boxing matches there. This was not considered a ladylike activity. Anna, however, was not concerned about being ladylike. Unlike some of her classmates, she didn't play the part of the sweet, helpless female when male students visited from nearby colleges. In fact, she earned the nickname "The New England Refrigerator" because of her cool behavior toward some of the young men she met.

As Anna's life was changing, the United States was changing, too. The nation and its cities had been growing rapidly for years. More and more forests were being cut down to make room for settlements. Wild animals were being hunted so intensely that some species were dying out. Since the late 1800s, people such as John Muir had spoken out in favor of **conservation,** or the protection of wild places and wildlife. During Anna's college years, Theodore Roosevelt, a conservationist and an amateur naturalist, was president. By establishing new national forests and wildlife preserves, Roosevelt did more to protect wild lands than any previous president had. Soon, many people were taking trips to places like the Grand Canyon and Yellowstone National Park, learning to appreciate the wonders of nature.

Things were also changing for women, who began to experience new freedoms. Some worked in factories, earning more money than they could have before. Others, like Anna, went to college. Women could join mountaineering groups like the Sierra Club, just as men did. But they still did not have the right to vote. Many women, especially on college campuses, began to be more vocal in demanding this right.

Anna at Cornell

It was an exciting time, but Anna wasn't excited about her schooling. Though she was a bright student, she struggled with a math class and eventually had to drop the course. She just didn't seem to fit in at Wellesley. Anna didn't give up on her education, though. A Wellesley instructor suggested that she enroll at Cornell University in Ithaca, New York. Cornell was a fairly new university that was attended by both men and women. It offered a freer atmosphere than Wellesley in several ways. Like the Morgans' farm, Cornell was surrounded by open land. Even better, the university attracted students and professors who shared Anna's love of nature. The college boasted an agricultural experiment lab and an insectory, a place where scientists could raise and study insects. It also had the best natural studies program in the country.

Anna started at Cornell in 1904, majoring in **zoology,** the study of animals. She thrived in her new environment. She took a fascinating course in **entomology,** the study of insects, with John Henry Comstock, an expert on insects and other tiny creatures. Professor Comstock's wife, Anna Botsford Comstock, was an excellent nature artist and teacher who offered Anna an example of what women could accomplish in science.

Pond Partners

Like Anna, you can try to find others who share your interest in aquatic life. Have you noticed other kids poking their noses into puddles or investigating babbling brooks? Try suggesting an expedition to a local pond or stream (be sure to ask your parents for permission). Maybe you can share books or, even better, your ideas. If you don't know anyone who gets excited about searching for tadpoles or underwater snails, talk to your science teacher. There may be local clubs, such as 4-H or scouting organizations, that can help you learn about pond life.

When Anna graduated from Cornell in 1906, few jobs in science were open to women. But Anna soon landed a job as a teaching assistant at Mount Holyoke College, a prestigious college for women in South Hadley, Massachusetts. Mount Holyoke had a long tradition of teaching science, dating back to the days when Mary Lyon, the college's founder, had shared her love of physics and chemistry with her students.

This commitment to science had been carried on by Cornelia Clapp, the head of the zoology department. Clapp had studied at Mount Holyoke, where she was influenced by the teachings of scientists such as Louis Agassiz. Agassiz told his students to "study nature, not books"—an unusual idea at the time. For years, science had been taught almost solely from books. But schools like Mount Holyoke had laboratories where students could study live animals and dissect, or cut open and examine, dead ones. During the summers, Clapp even took her students to Woods Hole, Massachusetts, to study aquatic life at the seashore.

At Mount Holyoke, Anna found not only a women's school committed to scientific discovery, but also a mentor. Cornelia Clapp wowed her. She was brilliant and full of life, and her passion for studying living things matched Anna's. Under Clapp's leadership, Anna prospered. Years later, Anna wrote that the goal of education was to make people less lonesome in the universe. At Mount Holyoke, she found that she loved helping her students become less lonesome by investigating the life around them. She worked enthusiastically, and within a year she was promoted to the position of instructor.

During the summers of 1907 and 1908, Anna returned to Cornell to study insects. There she met James Needham, a professor of aquatic **biology,** or the study of living things. Needham was a water wizard. He had studied stoneflies, caddisflies, mayflies, damselflies, midges, and diving beetles. He even wrote an entire book about dragonflies. Anna later wrote that Needham "first showed me how to look for things in the water; since that time he has continually given me help and encouragement for finding more."

In 1908, with James Needham's help, Anna became one of the few women admitted to the Entomological Society of America. She knew that belonging to this organization would help her to form partnerships with other scientists and to publish articles about her discoveries. She would soon have plenty to write about.

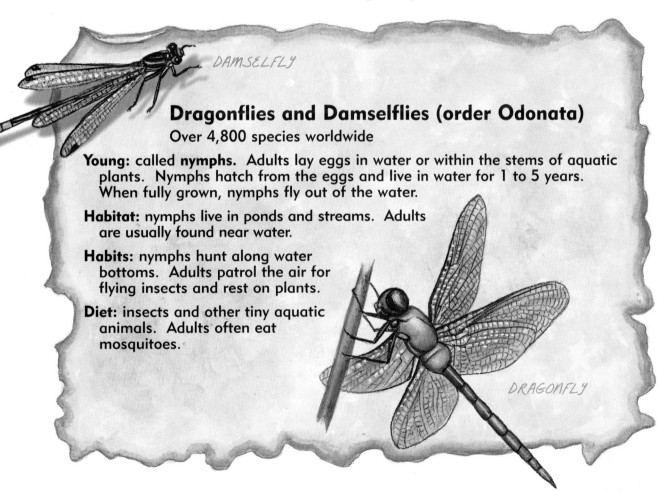

DAMSELFLY

Dragonflies and Damselflies (order Odonata)
Over 4,800 species worldwide

Young: called **nymphs.** Adults lay eggs in water or within the stems of aquatic plants. Nymphs hatch from the eggs and live in water for 1 to 5 years. When fully grown, nymphs fly out of the water.

Habitat: nymphs live in ponds and streams. Adults are usually found near water.

Habits: nymphs hunt along water bottoms. Adults patrol the air for flying insects and rest on plants.

Diet: insects and other tiny aquatic animals. Adults often eat mosquitoes.

DRAGONFLY

The Well-Equipped Water Watcher

Anna Morgan used many tools when she investigated the life of ponds and streams. A small aquarium net works well for scooping up critters from the water. A plastic container such as a yogurt or cottage cheese container will help you view your catch. With a magnifying lens, you can examine tiny life-forms in detail. A notebook is handy for jotting down discoveries and questions. To be a well-equipped water watcher, gather some of the items below.

backpack with notebook, pen or pencil, water bottle, and snacks

sun hat

aquarium net

field guide

magnifying lens

plastic containers

shoes or boots that you can get wet

Anna returned to teach at Mount Holyoke in the fall of 1908, but Cornelia Clapp could see how much Anna had enjoyed her studies at Cornell. Clapp often told her students, "If you want to do a thing there is no reason why you shouldn't." She encouraged Anna to live by these words by carrying on her studies at Cornell. With this approval, Anna left Mount Holyoke and returned to Cornell to study aquatic life with James Needham.

How to Use a Magnifying Lens

A magnifying lens allows you to look eye to eye with underwater creatures such as tadpoles and dragonfly nymphs. But the view might be a bit blurry if you don't know how to use the lens properly. Just follow the steps below, and soon you'll be having plenty of wild water visions.

✔ Hold the lens up in front of one eye and close the other. If you can't keep your eye closed by blinking, use your finger to hold the lid shut.

✔ Peer through the glass. Move toward the object that you want to check out, still holding the lens close to your eye. If the object looks blurry, move the lens closer or farther away until you can see clearly.

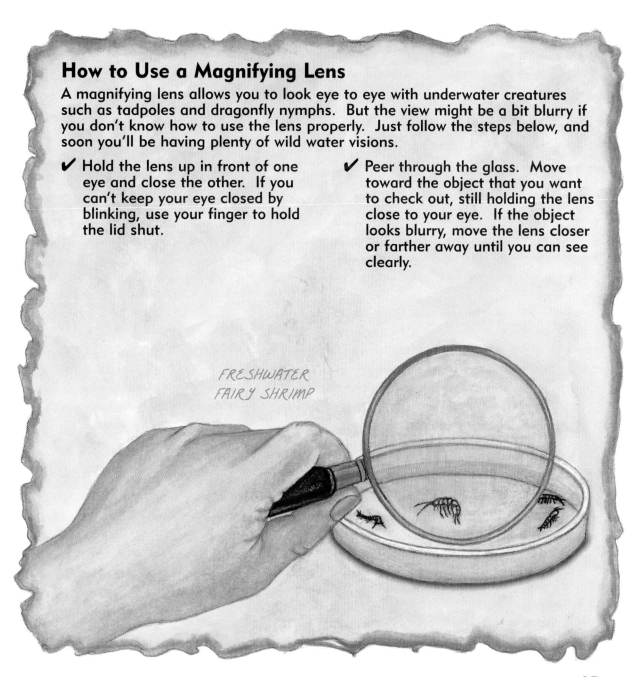

FRESHWATER FAIRY SHRIMP

Anna (lower left) studying water creatures with students at Cornell University

Chapter 3
Mayfly Morgan

At Cornell, Anna pursued the study of her favorite aquatic insect, the mayfly. She made friends with other students of freshwater life, such as Lucy Smith, who was studying stoneflies. To help pay her expenses, Anna also assisted in teaching younger students. She was so excited about her mayfly studies that before long, her students nicknamed her "Mayfly Morgan." Lucy was dubbed "Stonefly Smith," and together the two women inspired many students to study insects.

Like other naturalists, Anna had observed that living things have two main goals. All species strive to survive and to leave behind offspring. Anna was intrigued by the way that mayflies divide these duties into two extremely different periods in their lives. When a mayfly egg hatches, a tiny nymph emerges into the water. Nymphs are focused on surviving and growing. They quietly munch away on algae, other tiny plants, and microscopic animals. To get oxygen, the nymphs breathe through leaflike gills, organs that allow aquatic creatures to extract oxygen from the water. Scurrying on six legs through their underwater world, the mayfly nymphs continue to eat and grow for two months to three years, depending on the species.

Mayfly (order Ephemeroptera)

More than 2,000 species worldwide

Habitat: nymphs live in mud or under stones in ponds, streams, and rivers. Adults live in the air, resting in trees or shrubs.

Habits: spend most of their lives as nymphs. Live only a few days as winged adults out of the water

Diet: algae and microscopic plants and animals

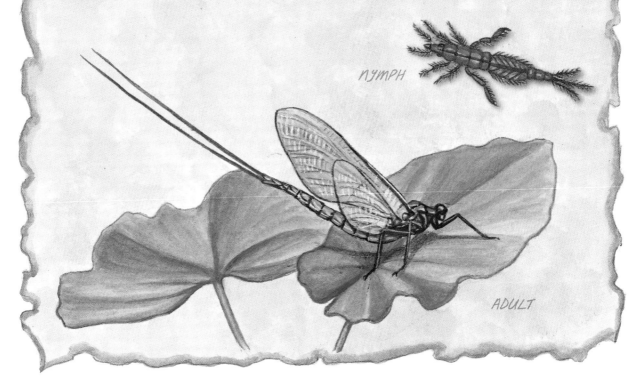

NYMPH

ADULT

When the nymphs are fully grown, they drift up to the surface of the water. There they slip out of their skins and pump out their large, veined wings. These dull-colored flyers are called subimagos. Within a day or two, they shed their skins once more and become shiny adults. They no longer have gills, so they can't breathe underwater. Even more amazingly, adult mayflies can't eat because their mouths are useless. Their one goal is to create offspring, so they fly about in search of mates. Soon after mating, the female deposits her eggs, and both the female and male mayflies die. The next generation hatches from the eggs, and the cycle of life and death continues.

Catch On

Would you like to catch, identify, and study aquatic animals from a pond or stream? Keep in mind that collecting animals and plants in parks and preserves is against the law. Contact your local parks department or natural resources department to find out where you're allowed to collect small aquatic creatures. (Look in the government section of the phone book.)

Supplies

✔ aquatic net
✔ plastic container
✔ magnifying lens
✔ notebook
✔ pen or pencil
✔ field guide

What to Do

✔ If you're visiting a pond, dip your container in the water. Examine the water you've collected, using your magnifying lens to focus on anything that moves.

✔ If you don't spot any creatures, try sweeping your net through the water. Search the net carefully. Small critters may be hiding in pond plants.

✔ Scoop up some mud with your net, then rinse the bottom of the net to thin out the mud. You may find tiny animals in the muck.

✔ Place any critters you find in your container and add some pond water.

✔ If you're searching a stream, pick up rocks and look under them. Stoneflies and other creatures that live in fast water hang out under rocks to stay safe from the current and hungry fish.

✔ Collect stream dwellers by placing your net in front of rocks before lifting them. The current will wash animals into the net. Scoop them into your container and add stream water.

✔ When you're done "fishing," place the container in the shade, so the animals won't get too hot. Examine them carefully with your magnifying lens. See if you can discover their identity using your field guide. For example, small, whirling red dots in pond water may be shrimplike animals called copepods. They could also be water mites, which look like tiny spiders.

✔ In your notebook, list all the species you find.

✔ Be sure to return your catch to its watery home when you're done with your investigation.

Fall Creek, where Anna hunted for mayflies, is well named. It starts as a gentle brook that flows past meadows, then plunges through a narrow gorge in a series of wild cascades. The creek has quiet pools, rippling shallows, muddy banks, sandy shores, and waterfalls. With these diverse habitats, it's no wonder that Fall Creek is home to a great variety of mayfly nymphs. Anna waded into the shallows and poked about cascades, collecting all the mayfly species she could find. She found nymphs clinging to the undersides of stones and clambering on piles of sticks and leaves. Others lurked in quiet waters or hid in shallows. There were even nymphs in mucky banks and white-water rapids.

Anna carefully examined each species of mayfly. She identified the nymphs and made detailed drawings of their characteristics. Most important, she began to notice the **adaptations** each species had made to its particular stream habitat. An adaptation is a change a species makes over time in response to certain living conditions. For example, a camel's hump, which stores fat, is an adaptation to the harsh, dry deserts where camels live.

It was easy to see that mayflies that lived in oozy mud were built differently than mayflies that dwelled in rapids, but how did these different body shapes help them survive? Anna studied a variety of species of mayfly nymphs, comparing the design of their gills with their habitat. She also compared mayfly eggs and investigated how various species collected food. These observations proved how well each species had adapted to its particular way of life.

Custom Gills

Anna learned that the gills of different mayfly species are similar in some ways. They're flat and have veins, so they look sort of like leaves. Tiny amounts of oxygen are absorbed all along the surface of each gill. But in other ways, gills are adapted to suit the needs of individual mayfly species.

✔ **Elephant Gills**
The nymphs of some mayfly species graze sluggishly along the leafy bottoms of ponds. These species have large, floppy gills that take in a lot of oxygen. The gills are cumbersome, but these nymphs are in no hurry.

✔ **Fast Flappers**
Nymphs that scurry about the still waters of ponds have smaller gills that are equipped with muscles. The nymphs can flap their gills rapidly to collect as much oxygen as possible.

✔ **Crud Filters**
Mud-dwelling nymphs have gill covers with a fringe of hairs. Their gills have hairs, too. When the gill covers are held against the gills, they form a filter that lets in water but strains out grit.

✔ **No-Slip Grippers**
Fast-moving rapids are rich in oxygen, but nymphs that live in these bubbly waters need to hold on tight to keep from being swept away in the current. Their gills have spines that help the nymphs cling to rocks.

Equipment Check

Checking out the special equipment on aquatic creatures can reveal a lot about their adaptations. To breathe underwater, some creatures use gills, while others carry air bubbles. Still others, such as mosquito nymphs, inhale through snorkel-like tubes. To move around, some water creatures use their legs as oars, some wiggle, and some walk on the surface. Others, such as dragonfly nymphs, shoot water to propel themselves forward. See what kind of aquatic adaptations you can spot in a local pond or stream.

Supplies
- ✔ aquatic net
- ✔ plastic container
- ✔ magnifying lens
- ✔ notebook
- ✔ pen or pencil

What to Do
- ✔ Collect some small aquatic creatures from a pond or stream where collecting is permitted. Place them in a plastic container with water from their home pond or stream.

- ✔ Watch the animals to see if you can figure out how they breathe, travel, and eat. Can you guess how their adaptations help them survive? Write down your theories and observations.

- ✔ When you're done viewing the animals, return them to their homes.

MOSQUITO NYMPH

As Anna's knowledge of aquatic insects increased, she learned that scientists weren't the only people interested in them. Fly fishers had plenty to learn from mayflies and their relatives. People who fly fish try to catch trout with "flies"—small replicas of insects made from feathers, hair, and yarn. The flies, which are attached to a hook and line, are made to look exactly like species of mayflies, caddisflies, or other insects that trout eat. Anna didn't fish herself, but she became fascinated with fly fishing. She knew her aquatic insects so well that it was easy for her to craft well-made flies for her friends who fished. Soon these friends learned about aquatic insects too, making them better able to catch trout.

Ann (left) with Cornelia Clapp in about 1913

Chapter 4
Electric Professor

In 1912, Anna finished her mayfly studies and returned to Mount Holyoke as Dr. Ann Morgan. (She had decided to shorten her first name.) At the age of thirty, she had earned a Ph.D., the highest university degree. At a time when very few women even attended college, she had proven that she could do detailed research. She had also inspired students at Cornell with her love of zoology.

For the next few years, Ann worked alongside Cornelia Clapp, first as an instructor and then as an associate professor. Ann lived on campus in a dormitory with other professors and students. In the dormitory, everyone—even the professors—helped cook and clean. Ann was so busy with her work that she found it a challenge to remember to be on time for meals.

Ann began making new friends among the faculty and students. One was Elizabeth Adams, a young woman from Pennsylvania. Elizabeth was ten years younger than Ann, but she possessed the same intense interest in learning. In 1914, after Elizabeth graduated with a degree in zoology, she became an assistant in the zoology department, then an instructor. She and Ann lived in the same dorm, and their friendship continued to grow.

Ann had also become close friends with Cornelia Clapp, who was impressed by her hard work and sharp mind. When Clapp retired in 1916, she recommended that Ann take her place. At the age of thirty-four, Ann became the head of Mount Holyoke's zoology department. The next year, her responsibilities increased in an unusual way. Nations in Europe had been fighting World War I for several years, and in 1917 the United States joined the conflict. Because thousands of farmers were sent to Europe to fight, the country grew short of food. To help, Mount Holyoke students and faculty planted, harvested, and canned crops during the summer. Ann participated in these efforts, along with teaching and leading the zoology department.

Elizabeth Adams in 1914

On top of these duties, Ann continued to study mayflies. She had been gathering mayflies for many years and had assembled one of the largest collections in the country. During Christmas break in 1917, a fire swept through Williston Hall, home to the zoology department's labs and collections. Ann's collection went up in smoke. Fortunately, she had already completed most of her drawings for John Henry Comstock's new book on mayfly wings.

Cornelia Clapp lost her huge collection of animal skeletons, but she remarked that a good fire had been needed to clear things up and she was glad to be rid of all that stuff. Ann knew her students didn't feel that way. They would have to study in crowded temporary quarters until a new building could be constructed. Still, Ann saw a blessing in the fire. The zoology department had needed a new laboratory for years, and at last the college would have to build one.

After the fire, Ann wrote to zoos all across the country, asking for help in rebuilding the zoology department's collections. Soon animal skeletons and carcasses began to arrive in the mail. Ann had the bones cleaned and assembled, and the zoology collection grew once more. She and the other professors also helped plan the new zoology building, which was named Clapp Laboratory. The lab's most interesting feature was an indoor stream environment that Ann created. It had a patch of woods, a mossy brook, and a pool that extended halfway down the hall.

Whether she was studying mayflies, harvesting crops, or lecturing to her classes, Ann's energy was boundless. One student described her as "electric." Even her thick hair often seemed to be charged with electricity. Ann was short in stature, but not in presence. Dressed in her lab coat and tie, she impressed almost everyone with her clear, crisp speech and vast vocabulary. Standing at the podium, blue eyes sparkling, she captivated her audiences with her creativity and wit.

Although Ann was a fascinating professor, she wasn't an easy one. "Let nothing come between you and your grasshopper," she would instruct as she directed her students in drawing. "Anyone can draw," she would say—and she accepted no excuses from reluctant artists. At Cornell, Ann had learned that drawing was a way to observe animals more closely. Sometimes her students would get so interested in their specimens that they would forget to draw, but she would urge them to record what they saw. In the process, more details would be revealed.

24

Picture an Aquatic Creature

Ann Morgan wrote many scientific articles throughout her career and illustrated most of them herself. Even if you aren't an artist, you can try sketching aquatic creatures, too. Remember that you don't need to create a masterpiece—just open your eyes and enjoy yourself!

Supplies
- ✔ aquatic net
- ✔ plastic container
- ✔ jar lid
- ✔ magnifying lens
- ✔ pencil or pen
- ✔ colored pencils or markers
- ✔ blank paper
- ✔ field guide

What to Do
- ✔ Collect an aquatic creature or two from a pond or stream where collecting is permitted. Place the creature, along with some water from its home, in a jar lid.

- ✔ Scan the animal with your eyes and magnifying lens. Make a mental list of all the parts, shapes, and colors that you can see.

- ✔ Try some quick sketches of a few of the creature's parts. Don't worry about how your sketches look—just draw.

- ✔ When you feel ready, sketch the basic shape of the entire animal.

- ✔ Add the animal's parts to your sketch.

- ✔ What colors can you see? Many aquatic creatures just look brown at first, but if you look carefully you may see different shades of green, yellow, or other colors. Try to match these colors with your colored pencils or markers.

- ✔ Write down any questions you have about your creature. Use your field guide to identify your subject after you've drawn it.

- ✔ When you've finished sketching, return the animal to its home.

Pond Snail

Ann (right) and Elizabeth in Woods Hole, Massachusetts

Ann's classes were exciting, especially for her many city-dwelling students who had never waded into a stream to look for caddisflies or hiked to a pond to study turtles. Ann's favorite place to take students to conduct research was a pond on nearby Mount Tom. She even went there in the winter and chopped holes through the ice to gather the water bug traps she had placed there. Ann also grew to love the Marine Biological Laboratory in Woods Hole, Massachusetts, where she began spending summers in 1918. There she taught students about starfish, sea urchins, and other spiny ocean-dwelling creatures.

The 1920s began with a big change for women. In August of 1920, Congress passed the Nineteenth Amendment, giving women the right to cast ballots in elections. Ann was thirty-eight years old, and for the first time she could vote. The next summer, she joined her friend Elizabeth Adams to conduct research at Yale University, where Elizabeth was working on her Ph.D. But it was in 1926 that Ann had a real summer adventure: a trip to the tropical jungles of British Guiana, in South America, where she did research on a remarkable insect called the stump-legged mayfly.

Ann began her work by finding a mucky area near a stream, a likely place for mayflies to live. Late one evening, she ventured out to the stream bank. With a spotlight, she scanned the sky and spotted a ghostly-looking swarm of adult stump-legged mayflies. Confused by Ann's light, they began plummeting to the ground at her feet, where they remained, helpless. She watched them fall for thirty minutes, until the last one had dropped.

When Ann examined the females, she saw that true to their name, they had only stumps for legs. The males had long front legs, but their other legs were short, like those of the females. Without working legs, adult stump-legged mayflies had to rely on their wings. If they landed, they would be unable to walk or even take off again. But the inability to walk didn't normally matter much to the stump-legged mayfly. The only purpose of its adult life was mating, which occurred in the air. Because legs weren't necessary, over many generations they had gradually shrunk into stumps.

For years, Ann had been intrigued by the way the mayfly's life is divided into distinct phases of growth as a nymph and reproduction as an adult. The stump-legged mayfly turned out to be an amazing example of that trait. The body parts it didn't need for reproduction had actually vanished over time! As Ann wrote in a report on her research, the male stump-legged mayflies had retained long front legs because they needed them to hold on to the female during their brief mating flights.

Egg Hunt

On a visit to a pond or stream during the summer, you may be able to spot aquatic insects mating and laying eggs. You may see clouds of midges or mosquitoes hovering over shrubs, damselflies cruising along together, or water striders riding piggyback on the water's surface. After these winged insects mate, the female deposits her eggs. Some species lay their eggs on plants, others in floating rafts. Dragonfly eggs are dropped into the water like torpedoes from an airplane. See if you can find insect eggs along the edges of ponds or streams, on aquatic plants, or on underwater stones.

Summer research was indeed exciting, but Ann had also grown fascinated with the behavior of animals in winter. How did frogs and mayflies survive for months in frozen ponds? Did snow and ice help or harm creatures such as turtles and snakes? In the winter of 1928, Ann decided to study the effects of winter on one of the simplest animals, the freshwater sponge.

Like artificial kitchen sponges, freshwater sponges are full of small holes that are linked together by an intricate series of tiny tunnels. But unlike a kitchen sponge, a freshwater sponge is a living animal. Sponges have skeletons but not arms, legs, or organs. They grow in groups called colonies on sticks, stones, and other objects found in the water. A single colony is composed of so many individual sponges that they're hard to count. Each fall, sponge colonies shrivel up, leaving behind buds called gemmules. In the spring, new colonies grow from these buds.

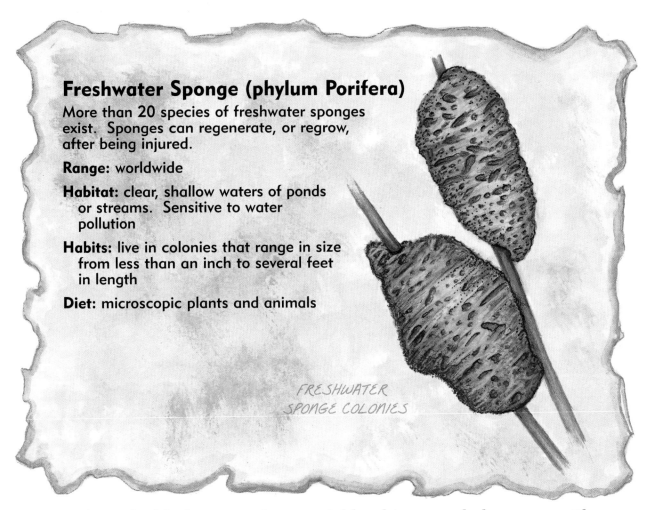

Freshwater Sponge (phylum Porifera)

More than 20 species of freshwater sponges exist. Sponges can regenerate, or regrow, after being injured.

Range: worldwide

Habitat: clear, shallow waters of ponds or streams. Sensitive to water pollution

Habits: live in colonies that range in size from less than an inch to several feet in length

Diet: microscopic plants and animals

FRESHWATER SPONGE COLONIES

Ann decided to test how quickly this growth happens. She scraped some gemmules from a rock in a frozen winter stream and set them in a dish of water inside a warm room. Using a magnifying lens, Ann observed and recorded the changes that took place. The gemmules began to swell and crack open on the third day. A day later, white streams of sponge cells came through the cracks. By day five, small sponge colonies were growing around each empty gemmule shell. Within two more days, the colonies had grown together into one large colony. Through this simple investigation, Ann discovered how quickly sponges are able to respond to changes in water temperature.

A few months after Ann completed her sponge study, her friend Elizabeth Adams returned to Mount Holyoke. She had earned her Ph.D. and was ready to join the Mount Holyoke zoology department as an instructor. Like Ann, Elizabeth became a popular teacher, and the two naturalists continued to share both their ideas and their companionship.

Chapter 5
Little Books, Big Ideas

Ann's first book, *Field Book of Ponds and Streams,* was published in 1930. The source of her inspiration was obvious from the field guide's introduction. "This book began in ponds and streams where frogs sat on lily-pads and by swift brooks where mayflies flew forth at twilight. It originated where water plants and animals live and I hope it will be a guide into the vividness and variety of their ways."

The book's 448 pages were packed with information about aquatic animals and plants—everything from leeches to lampreys. Readers could learn how to make nets and even a freshwater aquarium. Ann had worked on the book for several years, squeezing in writing sessions during the summer and whenever she could. Many zoologists and biologists had helped her, but she dedicated the book to her best friend, Elizabeth.

Field Book of Ponds and Streams became an immediate success. Never had so much information about freshwater aquatic life been available in one volume. Although the book was long, it was compact, so it could easily be taken into the field. It inspired teachers, amateur naturalists, and fishers to look more closely at ponds and streams. The book was reprinted in several languages, and Ann received letters from readers all over the world. She thought it was "great fun" to hear from people who appreciated her work.

Mini Aquarium

Would you like to host small pond animals in your home? In her *Field Book of Ponds and Streams*, Ann Morgan described how to make a balanced aquarium. Animals (including people) breathe in oxygen and breathe out carbon dioxide. Plants take in carbon dioxide and give off oxygen. By keeping plants and animals together in a small aquarium, you can maintain a balance of the oxygen and carbon dioxide that your aquatic guests need to survive.

Supplies
✔ aquatic net
✔ plastic containers
✔ two cups of mud
✔ two cups of sand
✔ clear plastic tub (one gallon or larger) or small fish tank
✔ notebook
✔ pen or pencil

What to Do
✔ Wild plants cannot be collected in many places without a permit. So the best way to get plants for your aquarium is to visit a pet store. Purchase a few freshwater plants such as elodea. They should cost no more than a few dollars.

✔ Collect some small pond creatures and a few quarts of pond water from an area where collecting is permitted.

✔ Spread a layer of mud on the bottom of the plastic tub or fish tank. Spread the sand on top of the mud.

✔ Set the plants you purchased in the layer of sand and mud, covering the roots gently. Add the pond water, being careful not to stir up the sand and mud.

✔ Add the aquatic critters you've collected. Where do they go? Do they try to hide among the plants? Make notes about what you see.

✔ After a few days of observation, return the animals to their home pond. **Warning:** Do not put any store-bought plants into ponds or streams—they may harm the native wildlife.

As Ann approached the age of fifty, she felt that it was time to have a home of her own. Living in Mount Holyoke's dormitory was like being at work all the time. A house would provide privacy and a place to entertain friends. Elizabeth felt the same way, and the two of them decided to build a house a short distance from the college. They chose a site that overlooked Mount Tom and a beautiful green valley, with the Connecticut River shimmering in the distance. In 1932, the house was completed. Ann and Elizabeth filled their home with books and a collection of paintings, and they each had a study.

In this cozy new house, Ann and Elizabeth often held meetings with their students. To many of the young women, the two professors seemed like older sisters. Ann listened earnestly to their concerns, problems, and ideas. She coached them through difficult times and helped them find jobs after college. But Ann could also act as youthful and silly as any eighteen-year-old. Sometimes she discussed clothes with the younger women, and one day she joked that she was "going in strong for painted nails and lipstick"—fashions of the younger generation.

Ann and Elizabeth's house

Ann assists a student in Mount Holyoke's zoological laboratory.

Despite her kidding, Ann continued to dress plainly and practically. In fact, she was often seen knee-deep in a stream, wearing hip waders and a broad-brimmed hat. She didn't mind looking different from most women. And although Ann was devoted to her students, she also showed her feelings clearly when she was annoyed with them. Because she dressed as she wished and spoke her mind freely, some students thought that Ann acted too much like a man. They noticed how different she was from Elizabeth, who was kind, pleasant, and ladylike. But others looked up to Ann for her independence and tried to be like her.

In 1933, Ann was one of three women listed among 250 leading scientists in *American Men of Science.* This was unusual recognition for a woman at that time, and as a result Ann was interviewed by *Time* magazine. She was becoming known throughout the country, and in South Hadley practically everyone recognized her. Even the men who drove the trolleys that Ann took to the pond on nearby Mount Tom referred to her as the "water bug lady."

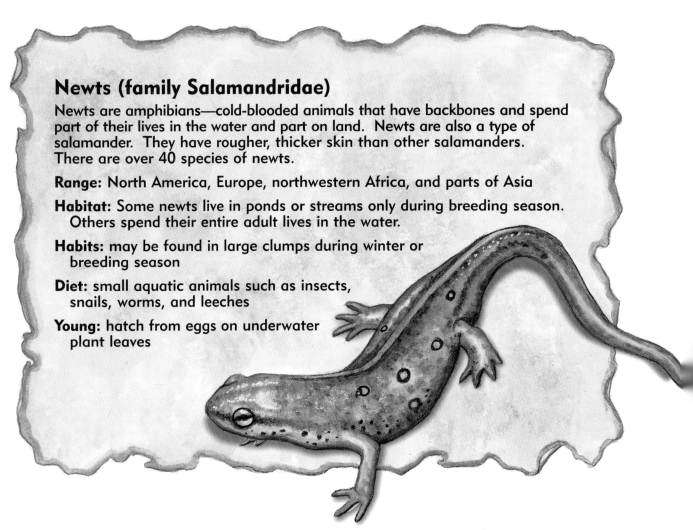

Newts (family Salamandridae)

Newts are amphibians—cold-blooded animals that have backbones and spend part of their lives in the water and part on land. Newts are also a type of salamander. They have rougher, thicker skin than other salamanders. There are over 40 species of newts.

Range: North America, Europe, northwestern Africa, and parts of Asia

Habitat: Some newts live in ponds or streams only during breeding season. Others spend their entire adult lives in the water.

Habits: may be found in large clumps during winter or breeding season

Diet: small aquatic animals such as insects, snails, worms, and leeches

Young: hatch from eggs on underwater plant leaves

By this time, Ann's curiosity about the winter life of aquatic creatures had led her into fascinating new research. Ann and her students studied beetles, mayflies, newts, and other animals. They learned that some animals, such as water fleas, die when cold weather arrives, leaving behind eggs that hatch in the spring. Others, such as frogs and groundhogs, enter a type of sleep called **hibernation.** A hibernating animal's body temperature drops, reducing its need for food and oxygen.

Ann learned that some animals remain active or somewhat active throughout winter. She observed newts creeping along stream bottoms even in January, feeding on mayfly nymphs and shedding their skin. When not active, the newts clustered in groups of twenty to forty, hiding beneath flattened stones and on the stems of an aquatic plant called chara. When Ann dissected the newts, she found that many had food in their stomachs, meaning they had eaten recently.

34

In 1939, Ann published her second book, *Field Book of Animals in Winter.* No one else had written anything like it. At last, people who wanted to explore nature during winter as well as summer had a guide to help them learn more about the lives of animals. The book described the different ways that animals survive the challenges of winter. It also gave specific details on how to locate and identify small creatures such as insects and snails, as well as larger animals such as turtles, squirrels, and ducks. For example, painted turtles can be recognized by their skin, which has yellow stripes and ranges from olive green to black, and by their shells, which may have red markings. In autumn, they burrow into the mud of ponds and quiet streams. They rest there, absorbing oxygen from the mud, until the water warms up again in the spring.

Painted Turtles (*Chrysemys picta*)

The painted turtle is one of more than 90 species of pond and marsh turtles. Turtles are reptiles, cold-blooded animals that have backbones and scaly skin. For protection, most kinds of turtles can pull their head and legs into their shell. They are toothless but have sharp jaws.

Range: eastern and northern United States and southern Canada. Some live in parts of the western United States.

Habitat: ponds, ditches, marshes, small lakes, and slow-moving streams

Habits: often bask in the sun in groups

Diet: water plants, insects, spiders, earthworms, small fish, frogs, and tadpoles

Young: hatch from eggs

Size: 4 to 10 inches

Seasonal Survey

With a sharp eye and a little patience, you can produce your own field guide of the seasons. All you need to do is keep track of the animals you find in your local ponds and streams at different times of year. **Warning:** Make your seasonal survey with an adult's help. Never venture onto ice-covered ponds or streams without supervision.

Supplies
✔ notebook
✔ pen or pencil
✔ field guide

What to Do
✔ Check the same pond or stream every month throughout the year. Use your field guide to identify the creatures you see, then record their names and the date in your notebook.

✔ In wintertime, look for resting critters in the mud and sand, as well as under stones. Jot down notes on the behavior of the animals you find.

✔ As the seasons go by, compare your observations. Soon you'll unravel the seasonal lifestyles of your aquatic neighbors.

As head of the zoology department, Ann was responsible for continually improving courses and offering new ones. One of her classes focused on freshwater **ecology,** the study of how living things interact with each other and their environment. At that time, most scientists didn't look at the connections between living and nonliving things, so they didn't always see the big picture in an environment. For example, many types of fish depend on insects such as mayflies, caddisflies, and stoneflies for food. If flooding or water pollution affects the population of insects, the fish will have less to eat and may die. This in turn affects the animals that eat the fish.

Ann was fascinated by the way ecology combined small details with the big picture. Her ecology-based class was one of the first offered at a college. Besides a weekly lab and field trip, each class did special projects. In teams of two or three, students studied outside at ponds or streams and then wrote reports on their discoveries. It was not easy work, but Ann's students found it exciting. Other colleges paid attention to Ann's teaching, and soon they too offered classes with an ecological approach.

Ann (second from left) shows students how to net pond creatures.

Chapter 6
Conservation of the Mind

Ann shared the big picture with her students whether she was discussing zoology or world affairs. In 1941, the United States entered World War II, which had been going on for more than two years in Europe, Asia, and Africa. Ann took time in her beginning zoology class to give students the historical background leading up to the war. As they had during World War I, students and faculty tried to help with the war effort. They mailed food, clothes, and books to Great Britain, one of the United States' allies in the war.

Ann found an unusual way to do her part. In 1944, she was asked to serve as an aquatic biologist for the Massachusetts state government. Because the country was short on food, one of her first duties was to survey the food supplies in Massachusetts lakes. Next, during the summer of 1945, Ann identified the food in the stomachs of about seven hundred fish taken from Massachusetts lakes. The survival of the fish depended on the health of the aquatic insects that they ate, so it was important to learn what their meals were like.

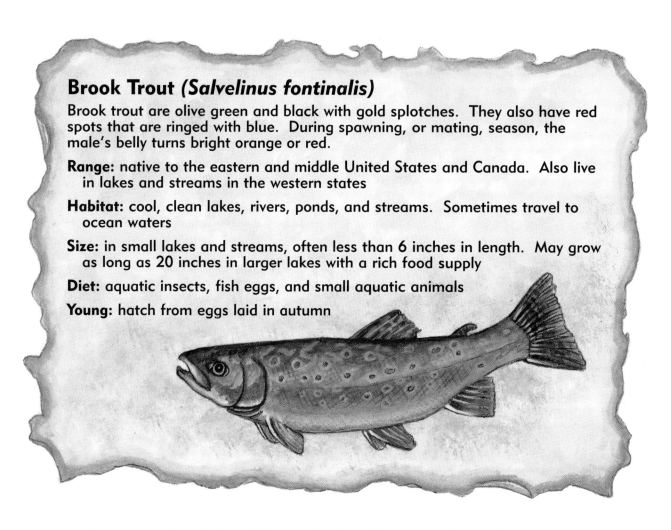

Brook Trout (*Salvelinus fontinalis*)

Brook trout are olive green and black with gold splotches. They also have red spots that are ringed with blue. During spawning, or mating, season, the male's belly turns bright orange or red.

Range: native to the eastern and middle United States and Canada. Also live in lakes and streams in the western states

Habitat: cool, clean lakes, rivers, ponds, and streams. Sometimes travel to ocean waters

Size: in small lakes and streams, often less than 6 inches in length. May grow as long as 20 inches in larger lakes with a rich food supply

Diet: aquatic insects, fish eggs, and small aquatic animals

Young: hatch from eggs laid in autumn

Ann's studies helped her to judge the overall conditions of the lakes and the fish that lived in them. For example, Ann confirmed that brook trout were becoming scarcer every year because of over-fishing, water pollution, and other changes that people caused in aquatic habitats. As she studied fish in Massachusetts and other states, she earned a new nickname—the "big fish lady."

Ann's work throughout New England made her aware that ponds, streams, and lakes were becoming more and more polluted. Aquatic animals are like pollution alarms. When water becomes even slightly polluted by factory wastes or sewage, animals such as stoneflies and sponges begin to die. To the untrained eye, a stream may look clean, but the destruction of life may have already begun. Once smaller animals die off, fish and other larger animals lose their food supplies. If nothing is done, most aquatic life eventually disappears. Zoologists who keep track of sensitive creatures like stoneflies are the first to see the results of pollution, so they can warn others to halt the contamination of water.

Though many people thought that studying nature was just a silly pastime, Ann knew that human beings depend on healthy natural systems for clean water and nutritious food. She believed that if people understood the dangers to wetlands, they would find ways to save them. In the late 1940s, Ann decided to spread the word to teachers and wildlife experts, who would in turn tell others. She began teaching a series of summer lectures on ecology and conservation in Connecticut and Rhode Island.

As she had done at Mount Holyoke, Ann taught outdoors, encouraging students to join her in the muck of ponds and streams, to experience nature with all their senses. The students learned to recognize aquatic creatures, but even better, they became aware of the changes that threaten wetlands. Ann hoped that courses like hers would lead not only to the conservation of wildlife, but also to the "conservation of the mind"—helping people to find peace by thinking about and better understanding the world around them.

Protect Your Watershed

Whether you live in a city or out in the country, you live in a **watershed.**
A watershed is an area of land in which snow and rainwater drain into the
same network of ponds, lakes, marshes, streams, and rivers. Changes that
occur in a watershed affect the water and the creatures that live in it. For
example, if too many trees are cut down, soil can wash into streams and lakes,
making them uninhabitable.

   You can help other concerned fans of aquatic life protect your watershed by
joining a local conservation group. To learn more and to see a map of your
watershed, visit http://www.epa.gov/surf/adopt/index.html and surf through the
Adopt Your Watershed Website.

In 1947, Ann was sixty-five years old. After forty-one years at Mount Holyoke College, she was finally ready to retire from the rigorous schedule of teaching classes and running the zoology department. Elizabeth Adams took over as head of the department, and Ann was free to energetically pursue her interests in ecology and conservation. That year, she attended the conference of the American Ecological Society and became a member of a national committee on conservation education.

Ann continued to speak out to those around her about threats to New England's wildlife. "Right here in the Connecticut Valley there are local conservation problems. Water pollution is one problem and overhunting and fishing is another," she told a newspaper reporter in 1949. Later that year, Ann and Elizabeth took a long tour of the Pacific coast to learn about conservation programs there. Ann was intrigued to learn that the western states were working hard to preserve forests and wildlife, and she brought many ideas home from the trip.

BULLFROG
TADPOLE

BULBOUS RUSH

Ann also kept writing about the natural world. In 1955, *Kinships of Animals and Man* was published. This book was a zoology textbook, but unlike other textbooks of the time it presented a broad, ecological picture of the study of animals. In it, Ann wrote that people should live in harmony with other life on Earth. "Now that the wilderness is almost gone," she wrote, "we are beginning to be lonesome for it. We shall keep a refuge in our minds if we conserve the remnants."

Ann continued to take nature photos, as she had done for years. She exhibited them at Mount Holyoke Art Center and at Cornell. The subject of many of her pictures was, of course, water. There were pictures of brooks, ponds, ice patterns, and rainy landscapes. Ann also took many scientific photos, such as mayfly nymphs shedding their gills and aquatic insects taking off on their first flights.

When Elizabeth retired in 1957, the two professors finally had time to slow down. One of their favorite pastimes was to take drives in the country. On special occasions, Ann would still visit the pond on Mount Tom. In 1962, Elizabeth had a heart attack, and she died soon after. Although Ann had many friends living nearby who could check in on her, she found herself living alone for the first time in many years.

Ann still had several projects to finish, including a book for fishers about aquatic insects and a biography of Cornelia Clapp, but she was finding it hard to work. She had begun to forget things, and her mind didn't seem to be as sharp as before. Sometimes when she went out, she would even get lost on the way home. Still, Ann didn't lose her sense of humor. One day a young clerk at a book-store was approached by a small, elderly woman who asked for a book about aquatic insects. The clerk offered Ann Morgan's *Field Book of Ponds and Streams* and explained its special features. But when the clerk added that the book cost five dollars, the customer exclaimed, "What! Five dollars for that little book! Why, it isn't worth anything like that!" Indignant, the clerk described in detail how unusual the book was and said it was worth far more than five dollars. The elderly customer laughed and gave the clerk a pat on the shoulder. "I am Ann Morgan," she said. "Thanks for the nice recommendation of my little book."

Ann died of cancer on June 5, 1966, at the age of eighty-four. She left behind money to establish a scholarship to support the studies of young women in science. It was called the Elizabeth Adams–Ann Morgan Fellowship. But Ann's most important legacies were her writings and teaching. She had influenced generations of young people to study freshwater life. As one student wrote, "To have her as a teacher even for one year was to have her live with you always."

Have you been hopelessly hooked by watery explorations? Maybe you've made friends with slippery garter snakes and whirling whirligig beetles. Like Ann Morgan, you may be anxious to explore and protect your local ponds, streams, and rivers. You too can become a pioneer in helping people understand and love the planet we call home.

GARTER SNAKE

Important Dates

1882—Anna Haven Morgan is born on May 6 in Waterford, Connecticut.

1900—Graduates from Williams Memorial Institute

1902—Enters Wellesley College

1904—Enters Cornell University

1906—Graduates from Cornell. Begins working as a teaching assistant at Mount Holyoke College

1907—Promoted to instructor at Mount Holyoke

1909–1912—Studies in graduate program at Cornell University. Changes first name to Ann

1912—Receives Ph.D. from Cornell. Returns to Mount Holyoke to teach

1921—Spends summer at Yale University with Elizabeth Adams

1926—Spends summer doing mayfly research in Kartabo, British Guiana

1930—Publishes *Field Book of Ponds and Streams*

1932—Builds house with Elizabeth Adams

1933—One of three women included in *American Men of Science*

1939—Publishes *Field Book of Animals in Winter*

1947—Retires from Mount Holyoke

1955—Publishes *Kinships of Animals and Man*

1962—Elizabeth Adams dies

1966—Dies on June 5

Glossary

adaptation: a change that living things make over long periods of time in response to their environment

aquatic: dwelling in water

biology: the study of living things

conservation: preserving and protecting natural life and habitats

ecology: the study of how living things interact with each other and their environment

entomology: the study of insects

hibernation: a type of sleep that some animals enter in winter

naturalist: a person who studies nature

nymph: a stage of growth some types of insects go through. Nymphs hatch from eggs and live in water until they grow to adulthood.

species: a type of animal or plant with common traits, especially the means of creating young

watershed: an area of land in which snow and rain drain into the same bodies of water

zoology: the study of animals

Bibliography

Alexander, Charles P. "Ann Haven Morgan, 1882–1966." *Eatonia* 8 (February 15, 1967): 1–3.

"Best Women." *Time,* March 1933, 38.

Bonta, Marcia Myers. *Women in the Field: America's Pioneering Women Naturalists.* College Station, Tex.: Texas A&M University Press, 1991.

Grinstein, Louise A., Carol A. Bierman, and Rose K. Rose. *Women in the Biological Sciences: A Biobibliographic Sourcebook.* Westport, Conn.: Greenwood Publishing Group, 1997.

Keene, Ann T. *Earthkeepers: Observers and Protectors of Nature.* New York: Oxford University Press, 1994.

Loewer, H. Peter. *Pond Water Zoo: An Introduction to Microscopic Life.* New York: Atheneum, 1996.

"'Mayfly' Morgan: 1882–1966." *Mount Holyoke Alumnae Quarterly* 79 (spring 1995): 68.

Morgan, Ann Haven. "A Contribution to the Biology of May-Flies." *Annals of the Entomological Society of America* 6 (1913): 371–403.

Morgan, Ann Haven. "Cornelia Clapp: An Adventure in Teaching." Mount Holyoke College Archives, South Hadley, Mass.

Morgan, Ann Haven. *Field Book of Animals in Winter.* New York: G. P. Putnam and Sons, 1939.

Morgan, Ann Haven. *Field Book of Ponds and Streams.* New York: G. P. Putnam and Sons, 1930.

Morgan, Ann Haven. "Fresh-Water Sponges in Winter." *The Scientific Monthly* 28 (1929): 152–155.

Morgan, Ann Haven. *Kinships of Animals and Man.* New York: McGraw-Hill, 1955.

Morgan, Ann Haven. "A Letter to the Alumnae." *Mount Holyoke Alumnae Quarterly* 31 (August 1947): 59–60.

Morgan, Ann Haven. "The Mating Flight and the Vestigial Structures of the Stump-Legged Mayfly, *Campsurus Segnis Needham.*" *Annals of the Entomological Society of America* 22 (1929): 61–69.

Morgan, Ann Haven. "May-Flies of Fall Creek." *Annals of the Entomological Society of America* 4 (June 1911): 93–119.

Morgan, Ann Haven. Papers. Mount Holyoke College Archives, South Hadley, Mass.

Morgan, Ann Haven, and Margaret C. Grierson. "Winter Habits and the Yearly Food Consumption of Adult Spotted Newts, *Triturus Viridescens.*" *Ecology* 13 (1932): 54–62.

Providence Sunday Journal, 8 July 1945.

Reid, George K. *Pond Life.* New York: Golden Books, 1967.

Richardson, Dorothy. "In Memoriam: Ann Haven Morgan 1882–1966." *Mount Holyoke Alumnae Quarterly* 50 (summer 1966): 93.

Springfield (Mass.) Union, 10 October 1949.

All quotations in this book are taken from the above sources.

Index